ISBN 978-0-259-80389-8
PIBN 10825599

Forgotten Books is a registered trademark of FB &c Ltd.
Copyright © 2018 FB &c Ltd.
FB &c Ltd, Dalton House, 60 Windsor Avenue, London, SW19 2RR.
Company number 08720141. Registered in England and Wales.

For support please visit www.forgottenbooks.com

THE TIGER

THE CALIFORNIA SCHOOL

of

MECHANICAL ARTS

Vol. VII   No. 1

SAN FRANCISCO

INDEX

The Mystery

WM. KOSTER HAKER, '10.

On the morning of June 14, 1907, the St. Louis Herald, fresh from the press, announced in big, bold headlines, the disappearance of Mrs. Scott's valuable diamond brooch. It appeared from the reporter's story, that Mrs. Scott, who was a wealthy society woman, had missed the brooch when she sought to wear it the evening before. As the brooch was a very valuable piece of jewelry, she was much alarmed at not finding it, but her husband pacified her by assuring her that it must have been mislaid, as she had not worn it for a week previous. A thorough search was immediately begun and every possible place was well looked over, and in her anxiety Mrs. Scott looked in many of the most improbable places, but the search proved fruitless. The servants were interviewed but they could shed no new light on the mystery. Suspicion, however, fell on the butler and he was promptly arrested, but as nothing could be proved against him he was allowed to go free.

The police were notified and private detective agencies employed, and these centered their energies on the case, finding it the most baffling they had had in recent years. Supposed clews were run down, but nothing was revealed. The case continued to be a mystery.

At the end of a month things had quieted down considerably, only to be stirred up more than ever by the startling announcement that the brooch was found, exactly as it was left, in the same drawer of the bureau from which it was originally lost. This discovery, instead of clearing the mystery only deepened it, and the Scotts continued the investigation through private detectives.

It developed that two nights before the reappearance of the brooch, on the night of the 16th of July, the family was out and nothing unusual was noticed by the servants. Also the drawer had not been opened between this time and the discovery of the brooch. It was evident, therefore, that the brooch was returned on the night of July 16th. All incidents of that date were recalled, and it was then that a maid remembered the finding of a small bit of paper in the hall while she was dusting on the morning of the 17th. The paper, which was a receipt for some chemicals bought of a certain chemist, she had burned up thinking it unimportant. The clue was followed up by detectives, and the chemist was located. His shop was in a remote portion of the city, and when questions were asked of him he recalled having been visited by a small, dark, smooth-shaven man with a scar over his left eye, probably due to a knife wound. The description was given to the police and a watch was kept throughout the city.

Nothing happened, however, until about a week later. A man answering the description pretty closely was seen to enter rapidly a dark alley but before he could be apprehended, he disappeared in one of the passageways. The place was shadowed by several detectives, and on the next night an entrance was forced where the man was supposed to have entered.

Detective Anderson, in charge of the case, led the way with his dark lantern and his hand on his revolver. One assistant followed closely. At the end of the passage they found a small door. Knocking brought no response, however, so the door was forced. It yielded without much resistance, being merely locked with an ordinary key.

The small, murky room into which they stepped contained only a rude table and one stool and a cot. The dark lantern further revealed a sooty lamp upon the table and a few newspapers lying around, and also at the furthest wall what appeared to be a door. The place showed signs of being hurriedly deserted, the occupant probably knowing that he was spotted. Anderson knew immediately that there was nothing in the room that was of value to them, so he went on to the inner door.

He found, however, that this door was heavier and more securely bolted than the first. It being fastened on the opposite side, there was no way to open it other than to force it. This was no light task. After repeated attempts, the door slowly gave way under the combined efforts of the two men. The inner room was pitch dark and to all appearances deserted. Flashing his lantern around, Anderson convinced himself that it was safe to venture further. Bidding his assistant to get the lamp, which was found still to contain some oil, from the other room, they soon had a light and found themselves in a small laboratory.

Arranged on a shelf, on the opposite wall, were numerous labeled bottles containing chemicals. Below this stood a heavy bench, on which was a pair of scales, such as used by jewelers in weighing small quantities; several bottles stood about and at the end of the bench was a small blast furnace worked by a foot bellows. A few mortars, test tubes and other apparatus commonly seen in a chemical laboratory were lying about in various corners of the room. There were no windows in the room and the only light must have come from the single gas jet above the bench.

Upon looking around more carefully Anderson found several small diamonds. These he carefully preserved; a small crucible, containing some crystals, that looked remarkably like the diamonds, was also unearthed in the furnace.

Anderson concluded that what he had before him were not diamonds, but counterfeits made by a clever rascal. The imitations were so good that no difference between them and the original could be discerned by the naked eye. They would not, however, stand a chemical test.

Anderson mused for several moments and was finally interrupted by his assistant, who said: "I fail to see the connection between this and the Scott case."

"Simplest thing out," replied his chief. "Our friend merely borrows jewelry, takes out the diamonds and substitutes his own fake-creations in place of them and returns the articles at the earliest opportunity, with some people none the wiser."

Randolph Watson

WILL R. BEATTIE, '10·

The winter wind howled mournfully, the great trees swayed and cracked, and peal after peal of thunder echoed and re-echoed, rolling out of the darkness of the night, made vivid now and then by the wicked flashes of lightning followed by torrents of rain which beat madly on the lone window of Watson's cabin. Within the cabin all was quiet save the ticking of an alarm clock and the occasional crackle of a stick in the fire. The furnishings of the cabin were scant—a rough wood table, two coarsely constructed chairs, a shelf, bed, and stove completed the list. On the table were dishes, barely enough for one person, and an array of spices, canned goods and the ticking alarm clock. On the shelf were grouped neatly a number of books, which on closer examination proved to be law volumes, political works and essays.

Watson sat near the stove with his back to the fire, in his hand a book which he read intently, stopping now and then to relight his pipe with a brand from the fire. As the light of the burning stick illumined his face it was found to be striking—a face which attracted and held the attention, not handsome but extremely out of the ordinary; a face you would not forget when once you had seen it.

The particular book which Watson was reading dealt with the life and political history of a famous "Boss." This particular paragraph was a brief outline of the college pranks and doings of the "Boss" when a youth, and as Watson read, it brought back memories of his own college days, his first leaving of home and the sadness of parting, his arrival at school and the terror of his first "Freshman" days, then the Sophomore and Junior years. He recalled the vacation before his Senior year, his trip to the old home, a full-fledged college man, and then—the girl; how he met and won her from his host of rivals, probably due to his college social training; how his flirtation, developed into love, and finally the parting when he again returned to school; how he longed for his sweetheart and planned on their future when he should graduate; and then the bitter news reached him that she had married another. He had left college, left his friends and his home, and come to the wilds of this mining country, struggling as only a desperate man can struggle until fortune favored him. His mine turned out to be the richest in the district. Wealth and luxuries were his had he desired them, but he had never forgotten the disappointment of his youth, and all the world held for him, even with his enormous wealth, was the rough mountain cabin and the life of a hermit, among the forests and mountains by day, and study at night. Thoughts of the woman who had been false were constantly upon his mind, had aged and hardened him until he had grown to regard mankind as his enemy. He took a peculiar delight in reading and studying the political issues, the struggle for wealth and the debauchery of public officials, receiving a sort of satisfaction in learning of the efforts and downfalls of human men. He delighted in society at war with ·itself.

Suddenly, as he read, a thought came to him. Why could not he, with fortunes at his command, enter the political arena and throw himself, body and soul, into the struggle? Crush and destroy? Plunder and—he stopped short. He had always been honest, always noble, had striven for high ideals, the good and truthful. But had not his life been blighted, his fondest hopes crushed and scattered at a blow? Again the hateful passion swept over him, and dashing the book to the floor, he sprang up and paced to and fro like a caged animal. Again his hatred of the human race dominated, and his desire to plunge into the battle increased.

Already plans were forming and shaping themselves in his mind. He became calm, and sitting down to the table, began to arrange his affairs. All night be worked while the storm without raged, seeming to goad him on in his relentless purpose. As the gray dawn approached, the storm relaxed in its fury, and with it the high nervous tension of the man relaxed. He slept soundly, his head buried in the mass of papers before him, and awoke to find the day well begun, leaving him only time enough to pack his belongings and catch the stage for the railway station.

PART II.

Randolph Watson sat in his luxurious city office and reviewed the events of the past few months. His success had been phenomenal, if aims accomplished through fraud and graft can be termed success. Immediately on coming to the city from his mountain exile, he plunged into politics, and aided by his wealth, his education and the knowledge of the political game acquired through nights of diligent study in his lone cabin of the mountains, he had steadily risen, but not without resorting to the lowest means of the profession. He had stolen his place by his cunning, had crushed and ruined honest men by the foulest of methods.

At the time of Watson's arrival, the city was in the grip of two "Political Bosses," each with power almost equal, and striving might and main, one to crush the other. Fortunes had been spent and lives and honor sacrificed in the relentless struggle. But neither would yield. As two struggling beasts of the forest locked in a death-grip, so were the two mighty factions locked, exhausted, each waiting for the other to weaken.

Watson, fresh, powerful, wealthy, held the destiny of each as a child holds a frail plaything. For a time he watched the struggle, until one side seemed to weaken, and then as the child would break the toy, he broke the deadlock—hurled the almost victorious faction to its death and was proclaimed the "Man of the Hour," with a seat in the city's council at his disposal.

He was now one of the two most influential councilmen and was ambitious to become mayor. This ambition ruled his life. When once the office of mayor was his, he could see vast opportunities, great and bewildering prospects for a future wherein power and mighty influence were his.

He lit a cigar and looked at his watch. Surely it was time for McEvoy to arrive. McEvoy was a lawyer, shrewd, skillful, who knew the political situation of the city better than any other man did; he understood the workings of the "inner ring" as no other man understood them, and he had been leagued with Watson, had aided and schemed with Watson from the first. The door opened and McEvoy was ushered in.

"Hello, Watson. I'm a trifle late, but my good news will compensate you for the delay." He drew a chair towards the desk and pulled from his pocket a bundle of papers.

"We have the mayor's office cinched. Only a matter of signing a few papers and the office is yours."

Watson would have risen, but was pushed back.

"Don't get excited now, old boy. Just keep cool and I'll show you how easy it is."

"Then for heaven's sake, Mac, hurry up; show. Your damned coolness would drive a man crazy."

Unfolding the papers, McEvoy began:. "You know your greatest enemy, Watson, is Hunt. He is almost as influential in the Council as you are. He can control more mayoralty votes than any other two put together, and if any man can keep you from getting the office he can; also, if any man can make it easy sailing for you, he is the fellow."

"Yes, but don't you ever allow yourself to think that he would help me."

"Hold on now, Watson. We have him in a place where he'll have to help you, providing you help him first. Will you do it?"

"Will I do it? You know my ambition, McEvoy. You know I am going to get that office at any cost. I am determined on it. Why, I'll shake hands with Hunt to-morrow, and I'll help him as much as is in my power. I will gladly do it if it can in any way aid me in my plans. What is your scheme?"

"Well, it's simply this: Hunt has a little deal on which will land him a millionaire provided he can get possession of a little strip of land adjoining the Gas Works on Fourth avenue. He has received inside information that the O. R. & S. are going to make their terminal in that vicinity, and if he can manage to obtain this property, together with what he now has, it will give him control of the entire situation, and he can set his own figure to the railroad company. However, the land is owned by a widow, and she absolutely refuses to part with it."

"Why don't he offer her a good sum?"

"He has, but she won't even consider it. It seems as if there is some sentiment attached to the thing."

"Well, what has all this got to do with me and the mayor's office?"

"Everything. Listen. I have just been over to Hunt's residence and he wants the Council to institute condemnation suit against the woman. Acquire the property—for him, of course, but making believe it is for the proposed enlargement of the gas plant. He has promised a rake-off to the fellows, and has succeeded in getting them all with the exception of you. He thought perhaps you would kill the thing because he was in it, if he approached you himself; so he phoned me to come over. I did so, and he told me what I have just told you. He said that if you would forget the past and vote the thing through as proposed, he would land you safe and sound in the mayor's chair next election. He is now waiting for your answer."

"It's a go, Mac. It's a go. I'll do it. Go and tell—or, hold on, I'll go with you."

Together they left the office and turned toward the home of Silas Hunt, Councilman.   (To be continued.)

The Mountains

BERTHA HARDER, '13.

How bewilderingly beautiful was the dawn! The sun gradually rose with increasing splendor, and slowly the valley below became visible. Pines, tall and stately, covered the mountain like a mantle.

A cataract sparkled in the rays of the sun, while its deep, thundering voice, as it dropped over rocky crags, echoed and re-echoed far and wide. The water fell far, far below to a dark pool which, overflowing, became a steady stream, rippling and murmuring in perfect harmony.

The day passed, and far in the west the sun left a red glow to mark his path. Sunset! Soon the moon appeared, and cast a silvery light over all. Nature seemed asleep, as,

> "Silently one by one,
> In the infinite meadows of heaven,
> Blossomed the lovely stars,
> The for-get-me-nots of the angels."

Two Democrats in the Fifteenth Century

[Editor's Note.—Miss Southwick spent last year in touring Europe and consented to write the following article from her experiences]:

"What are you going to call them? Marchioness rather sticks in my throat, I being an American. Does one kiss her hand?"

"He'll be more apt to kiss yours, he being an Italian gentleman! O, I suppose we shall just say 'Marquis' and 'Marchioness' every other minute for the next twenty-four hours! Why did we accept their invitation to their old country-place?" my friend wailed.

I sat up wearily and straightened my hat for the forty-ninth time. Third-class cars ride rather rough in Italy.

"Why," I replied bitterly, "didn't we expend another franc or two on a second-class ticket? I am afraid their man will cut us when we arrive from a third-class carriage, not to mention his feelings when he sees our luggage!"

"I only wish we'd stayed up till four instead of two o'clock and reduced the number of bundles somehow. An oilcloth roll, a teabasket, two wooden boxes of china—nice outfit! A credit to our national reputation for trim luggage and traveling light in America!"

"Yes, we look like a cartoon from life of an Englishman crossing the Rockies, all we lack is the tin bathtub. Have you the camera?"

My friend counted our hand luggage once more and found the camera under the seat.

"You take the alligator bag," she planned, "and the suitcase and hand it to the footman. I'll take the rest to the parcel-check place. If we must move in 'high societee' we'll do it with as little impedimenta as possible. Here we are."

"Don't leave me alone with any of the family," I begged. "Remember we can't say a word to each other. I'm so glad you know Italian. Don't look so sleepy, please!"

"O, the family won't be at the station. Don't you know in stories the nobility always send a dogcart to fetch their house-guests?"

"A hayrack would be more effective to meet us," I grumbled morosely, picking up one wooden box, the teabasket, the black oilcloth bundle and kicking my suitcase toward the door.

As I stumbled down the steps of our compartment like a laden packhorse descending a steep trail, the first sight that greeted my heavy, blinking eyes was the Marchioness herself, all smiles and nervous fidgets. Our disreputable baggage was seized and borne toward the station. Neither authority nor persuasion could induce the check-counter to accept packages so insecurely sealed or so fragile as Venetian glass. So, to our mortification, all our eight bundles were stowed in the carriage around the long-suffering feet of the Marchioness and of Mademoiselle, at our backs, between us even, and we were off. The stone pavements rang and clattered, the pedestrians hopped on the narrow curbings that serve for sidewalks and flattened themselves against protecting walls as we spun along the narrow streets. It was market-day but donkeys, oxen, even glittering officers a-horse, hastily gave us right-of-way. It was a novel sensation to see every one we passed saluting our august presence, but I was too embarrassed to enjoy this vicarious homage.

We had had a narrow escape a moment since. Only once before had we seen our host and hostess. Presented to them at a studio in Venice by some Americans they liked, we had been urged past all protesting to spend our last week-end in Italy at one of their palaces on our way to the homeward-bound ship. It was a rare opportunity to see an Italian interior. Let me remark that the hospitality shown us and the pains expended to guide us to every important sight are only typical of what the appreciative American may always expect at the hands of cultivated Italians.

But now we saw the Marquis for the second time and mistook him for the coachman, muffled as he was in driving coat and hat! Stepping to the side of the carriage to climb in, I caught a side-elevation of his face. No one could mistake that nose. My friend caught the cue as I shook hands and the situation was saved.

We tried hard as we passed along to look as if we were not uneasy at being guests of people whose titles go back to the days when America was not. I revolved methods of appeasing the Marquis who understood no English. I had no Italian. Evidently he liked horses. When we turned into the paved court of the stable and had been disinterred from our hand-luggage by footmen as skillfully as stevedores could have done it, I dashed to the heads of the horses and was sternly driven off by a groom. However, the host caught my eye and invited me into the stables by means of hospitable gestures. I was not at all sure whether he said the racehorse would or would not kick, whether I might pat him or no, but by means of difficult ejaculations, "Gia!" "Mache!" "Bello!"—and slapping the favorite on his best points, I held a successful conversation. As we went in for luncheon, I reflected that my one medium of communication, my one chance of being an appreciative guest, was now exhausted, and hoped my host would not find it in his duty to attend us on the afternoon's excursion to his country villa in the hills nearby. Doubtless he found it as trying to tact as I did to be entertaining without speaking, for we found only the Marchioness and Mademoiselle escorting us to the Castellnuovo della Bagni—a name much wider than the village—to visit one of the most famous examples of landscape gardening in Italy.

Never in this world do I expect to see anything more perfect than Villa Bellavista and its garden. A composite of all the pictures of Maxfield Parish, the pen of Mrs. Wharton or of Vernon Lee could scarcely do it justice. High on an olive slope hangs the villa. Its white facade and green blinds hide the village clinging to the mountainside above. Through an archway in the exact middle of the front and through the ample court, out under a loggia of a wing, passes the one cobbled street leading to the homes of the contadini beyond on the hill. Under the windows streams all day the varied life of northern Italy; panniered donkeys beside whom ragged boys toil and shout, workmen with gaudy red and yellow bandanas around their black heads, erect women bearing on their backs willow baskets full of greens and red tomatoes.

You would not want me to describe in detail, if I had the power, the cinquecento (fifteenth century) frescoes, the quaint embroidered hangings that matched the walls and ceilings in each room, or the beds, gilded, carved and curtained to carry out in color and design the escutcheons of various branches of the family. Every one of the fifty rooms would be interesting to an antiquary or an art-student.

Being neither, but a Californian, I most enjoyed the garden. It runs from the very foot of the hill up past the side of the villa to almost the crest of the rise. It marches up the hill by terraces, flanked by trees planted as only those Old World gardeners knew how to arrange, to accentuate the perpendicular lines. In the high light of the center is a great coat of arms worked out in suitable colors of glistening quartz and mineral stones. Beyond that are the marble balustrades of two stairways meeting in a wide sweep at each terrace. The whole framed in heavy foliage was brilliant with flowers in formal beds.

You can guess what visions haunted us there. Lorenzo and Jessica lived poetry in its fairy grottos. Portia paced among the cypresses conceiving a plan to save her lord from sorrow. Francesca da Rimini murmured, "I have wept but on the pages of a book." Whispers were in the air of

"Old, forgotten, far-off things
And battles long ago."

But even these terraces of carnations and lilies and greenery could take an added charm. The formal plots, straight rows, regular vistas and grand stairway, these were too cold for the ultimate touch of romance. Poetic memories borrowed from other Rennaissance Italian gardens left one unsatisfied. The one touch was supplied when our hostess signaled a gardener and keys were turned here and there. The place became alive with exquisite fountains.

At the top of the slope in the center stood a collossal white figure of a nymph. From a long trumpet she blew a graceful curve of water. Two great sons of Neptune below at her sides shot from their shell-like horns other streams to mingle with the cascades pouring from step to step down half the hillside. At each terrace two fountains jetted and played. Beyond the balustrades of the main terrace on the lowest level were two plain fountains that rose almost to the height of the nymph above and fell back sparkling and circling in broad round basins, happily breaking the stiff expanse. Is there any fascination like living water?

In the morning still another rare sight was ours. The unused rooms of the town house were opened for us to see. We were led through room after room of floors inlaid in wonderful patterns of marble and mosaic, of walls paneled with priceless old brocades; of hangings rich with the blazonry of two ancient lines; of painted ceilings, festooned and scrolled in faded reds and blues and greens, in all the fantasies of the Rennaissance; of oak and mahogany and walnut black with centuries and carved by master hands; of mirrors framed with the intricate gold garlands of the baroque period; rooms filled with furniture fit for a king to sit upon, Spanish leather and puntungaroo upholstery—it was the Italian palazzo of one's dreams. The settings of Crawford and Hewlett's tales became real before our eyes.

Costumes suitable in such a palace were not wanting when our hostess took us to a room full of tall wardrobes and began to shake out clothes worn at the court of Napoleon. Such brocade! Such satins! Such silks and velvets! Small clothes of "white samite, mystic, wonderful" in cut and tightness, long coats of long-napped green velvet sprinkled with golden fleur-de-lis, even a fan of the best French decoration,—one felt the atmosphere of that coquetting, minuetting, sword-fingering period.

When "the quiet-colored end of evening smiled" we had to bid good-by to a city that had charmed us to forget several centuries of time. On our way to the station we drove up a long incline to the top of the city wall. As we went its round we, like Browning's shepherd-lover, could see

"Where the domed and daring palace shot its spires
Up like fires
O'er the hundred-gated circuit of a wall
Bounding all,
Made of marble, men might march on nor be ,prest
Twelve abreast!"

Our walls were of ancient red brick; dull red too, the campanile pierced by exquisite white marble window-frames of Moorish style, one more in each successive story to give the requisite lightness as the square mass ascended. On the highest platform of one dull old tower grew an oak under which the 20-century owner was accustomed to give lunch-parties. Touched by "the tone of time" to a creamy whiteness was the facade of St. Martin's, built in the thirteenth century, with its vast portico of three magnificent arches above which are three ranges of open galleries, not one of whose delicate columns is like unto another in its exuberant carvings. The sun slanted rosily across a city of grim Roman arches and gray palace walls and red towers and cathedral marble, and touched it all to a city of dreams.

Our friends had brewed us a glowing stirrup-cup of memories as we set our faces toward the land of Promise. G. R. S.

Seeing Things

VIVIAN W. LAYCOCK, 1912.

Who said ghosts? Who ever saw such things? Yet, if you had been in Sam Keegan's shoes one night you might have seen them, for he did.

It all happened at a summer resort where people that really wanted a rest spent their vacations. It isn't often that two young girls would go to a place like that, but such was the case.

"Ethel, it is too hot to go to bed; so suppose we sit in the hammock for a while and cool off." This suggestion came from Valerie, the oldest of the two.

"All right, Valerie. I am willing, for I have nearly danced my feet off to-night. I think that bonfire and story-telling contest will be keen. Ghost stories are always interesting. Sam was telling me about it when we were dancing together. He was so interested in telling me how he wasn't afraid of such things that he almost forgot to dance, and I had to pull him around at the expense of having my toes stepped on."

"Do you know, I think that Sam Keegan would be more frightened if any one tried to scare him than we would be if a mouse should appear about now," commented Valerie.

"Or that crazy man."

"What crazy man?" asked Valerie, beginning to think of getting back to the hotel.

"Why didn't you hear Mrs. Reid telling about that fellow escaping from the insane asylum?" replied Ethel. "They say he imagines he is a ghost and he always wanted to wear sheets and pillow cases in the asylum."

"If Sam knew that he would not have been so anxious to walk home with Miss Williamson, up through those trees. It wasn't right for him to leave before the dance was over anyway." This from Valerie who rather liked him herself.

"You're just jealous," said Ethel.

"I'm not. Nothing to be jealous over."

"Wouldn't it be fun to hide some place and scare him when he comes back, if he ever does." With a sly look at her chum. "Our white dresses are just the thing."

"No, that would be mean."

"Oh, of course you would stick up for him," remarked Ethel.

"I'm not sticking up for him," retorted Valerie.

"Then if you are not come on and prove to me that you are not by playing the trick."

Valerie began to see that it would be quite a joke so she consented.

The girls had been swinging and the excitement caused by the idea of playing a trick upon poor unsuspecting Sam seemed to arouse them to such an extent they forgot their weariness. They had been sitting in the hammock longer than they realized, forgetting that Sam would probably take the short path coming back, so they busily planned how they would carry out their scheme.

"We will hide behind that old oak tree and jump out when he comes along," said Ethel.

"You are quite clever when it comes to devilishment, aren't you?"

"Yes," replied Ethel. "Especially when it is your friend."

With this the girls jumped from the hammock and ran toward the tree.

Poor Sam! He came upon them quite suddenly and seeing them swinging would have sworn they were ghosts flying through the air. Were they ghosts? Of course, and right where that hammock ought to be. These were the thoughts that ran through his mind. He didn't dare to even breathe. They must have heard him for they dropped to the ground and started after him.

Sam's first thought was to run, but no, that would never do. He wasn't afraid of ghosts. He didn't have to think twice before deciding, but turned in his tracks and faced those horrible phantoms. They stopped, uttered a heart-rending scream and fled, each taking a different direction. Sam not knowing which one to follow stood still. What did they want and why should they be afraid of a human being? Thoroughly disgusted with the cowards he turned toward the hotel.

By this time all was excitement at the hotel. The girls, white as ghosts they had pretended to be, came running in from different directions and all anybody could get out of them was, "Crazy man—fired—chased us," and other disconnected phrases. Something was wrong but in the excitement everyone had forgotten the escaped lunatic and all eagerly questioned the hysterical girls in the hope of finding the cause of the trouble.

Five minutes later when Sam entered the room he was more astonished than when the ghosts ran from him for both girls had grabbed him and were nearly tearing him to pieces. All that he could make out was that they thought he had been murdered and how did he escape from that crazy man. When the girls were finally quieted enough to explain matters Sam came near getting mobbed for laughing at the perilous adventure of the girls. He saved himself, however, by explaining that he was the crazy man and the girls were evidently the two ghosts he had seen.

"Now, Miss Ethel, maybe you won't be so willing to play one of your clever little tricks on anybody."

"Never mind, Miss Valerie, you would run too if you saw that you were in danger of having your toes stepped on again by the same party that had already danced the Barn Dance on them."

Both girls resolved to never again undertake the perilous task of impersonating ghosts.

Wireless Telegraphy

S. CLARK, '11.

The achievements and possibilities of wireless telegraphy are daily arousing public interest. Less than ten years ago, this magnetic wave phenomenon was first put to a practical use. The instruments and results obtained were, of course, very crude, but the progress since made has been rapid. New and more modern appliances are being almost daily invented. Where it was then possible to transmit and receive messages from fifty to a hundred miles, we are now able to transmit and receive messages very nearly three thousand miles.

This wonderful phenomenon has developed into an implement meeting a great necessity, and of utmost importance in maritime affairs. There is hardly a navy in the world of any importance that has not adopted wireless telegraphy, in some form, as an indispensable means of carrying on its transactions. Most of the large liners crossing either the Pacific or Atlantic oceans have a "wireless" equipment, which insures a greater safety of life and property, gives pleasure and makes a sea voyage more cheery and agreeable. Can you realize the comforts of being able to read a daily paper of the latest happenings when many miles out at sea or of engaging theatre tickets or a suite of rooms long before landing.

As a life-saver we may take the cases of the ill-fated ships Republic, on the Atlantic coast, and the Ohio, on this coast, whose passengers were saved from death just in the nick of time.

We have thus far seen only the practical side of "wireless." Let us now look at the theoretical side, a general idea of which may be procured from the following: it is a well known fact that when an alternating current of electricity is passed through a wire, periodic electro-magnetic lines of force are created, the strength of which depend on the strength of the current and the self-induction of the wire. These periodic lines of force are the path of magnetic waves which radiate in every direction with the speed of light, 186,000 miles a second, and when they hit upon or cut a conducting surface they induce an alternating current in it, of the same frequency as the radiator. Upon this the working of all "wireless" apparatus is based.

To produce these electro-magnetic lines of force, a transformer of a high potential is used. This transformer charges a condenser which, when charged to a certain potential, discharges through a circuit having concentrated self-inductance. When the discharge occurs, an alternating current of high voltage and frequency is formed, which alternates or oscillates in the circuit containing the spark-gap, across which the discharge occurs, condensers and concentrated self-inductance, entirely free of the transformer. This concentrated self-inductance has in most connections two uses: first, it only allows a current of a certain period of vibration to pass into the circuit which radiates the ether waves; secondly, it acts as the primary of a coreless step-up transformer which tends to make the oscillatory current formed of a still greater voltage. This inductance coil consists of a few turns of heavy wire, the ends of which are connected to the oscillating circuit. A slider or clip is fastened to a certain number of turns of the coil from both ends, the adjustment of which is termed "tuning."

To tune a station you first add enough inductance to the oscillating circuit to bring it into resonance with the charging current. Second, place the sliders or clips, one of which goes to the antenna or aerial and the other to the ground, so that there is sufficient inductance in the radiating circuit to make it act in resonance with the oscillating circuit. Now, when the telegraph key in the primary circuit of the transformer is pressed, the transformer starts charging the condenser. When the condenser reaches a certain potential, which is determined by the spark-gap, a discharge occurs. This discharge forms an oscillatory current, which is induced in the radiating circuit. The induced current forms periodic electro-magnetic lines of force around the wires of the antenna or radiating circuit. These lines of force create and are the path of the ether waves which are radiated into space as stated before. To make the different characters of the alphabet wave trains consisting of different amounts of oscillations with a pause between each are sent out; as for example, the character A is a very short wave train with a pause, then a longer wave train.

The receiving station is almost the same as the sending station. We have a coreless transformer or inductance coil the sliders of which go to the aerial and ground as in the sending circuit. In the place of the spark-gap we have a detector. The condenser, which is of a much smaller capacity, is placed in series with the detector and coreless transformer instead of in shunt with the transformer, as in the sending circuit. The detector is shunted with a pair of high resistance telephones and a battery. As a detector for wireless telegraphy, we have a great number to choose from. The detector that I will describe is called an electrolytic detector, because its action depends upon electrolysis. It consists of a very fine platinum wire barely touching a solution of any acid or alkali, which upon being electrolized, liberates oxygen and hydrogen gas. In the solution is a second platinum terminal of a larger size. The telephones and battery are shunted around the detector, so that upon electrolization, the oxygen will be liberated at the fine platinum wire. The battery current is then regulated so that just sufficient oxygen is formed to insulate the fine platinum wire. This is what is called critical potential.

When we wish to catch a station that is sending, we regulate the sliders or clips on the coreless transformer or tuning coil, such that the receiving station is in resonance with the sending station. The incoming wave cuts the aerial or radiating circuit and forms an alternating current in it. This current breaks down the film of oxygen bubbles on the fine platinum wire in the detector, thus allowing a current to pass, which is recorded in the telephones as a buzzing noise.

Thus, the principles of wireless, though marvelous to the uninitiated, can be easily explained so as to be understood by anyone having a fair knowledge of electricity.

THE TIGER

The Tiger is published everV quarter by the Students of the California School of Mechanical Arts (founded by James Lick), at 16th and Utah Streets, San Francisco, Cal.

Subscriptions—$1.00 per annum. Single copies, 25c.

Advertising rates upon application to Business Manager.

Entered as second-class matter August 22, 1907, at the post office at San Francisco, Cal., under the Act of Congress of March 3, 1879.

Exchanges address to C. S. M. A., 16th and Utah Streets, San Francisco, Cal.

REY E. CHATFIELD...Editor
SHERMAN A. WHITE..Manager

EDITORIAL STAFF.

MARGUERITE BOYD ....Literature
WILLARD R. BEATTIE...Literature
AGNES FRASER...School Notes
JOHN F. CORKER..School Notes
LAURENCE R. CHILCOTE...Technical
WILLIAM R. McNAIR..Technical
CLYDE A. PITCHFORD...Athletics
HERMAN B. HENDERSON...Athletics
ELSE BOYE...Athletics
WALTER DREYER...Exchanges
BERT R. DELERAY...Exchanges
ETHEL MAASS..Shop Notes
ELMER S. SPARROWE...Shop Notes
FRANK M. HOUSE..Shop Notes
FLORENCE REINHOLD...Joshes
ALLEN L. WETMORE..Joshes
CLIVE S. WINTER, Cartoonist..Joshes
W. W. BEATTY, '09..Alumni
C. S. SIMON, '09...Alumni
W. BOYD, '07...Alumni
CATHERINE BOYLE..PoetrV
WM. RICHARDSON..Art
ALICE SCHMELZ...Art
GEORGE N. SULLIVAN..Art
ALEXANDER H. BELL...Art

ASSISTANT MANAGERS.

J. D. BLACK, O. C. CAMPBELL, ALBERT T. MARGO, EDGAR MEYERINK, GEORGE E. MONTGOMERY, FRED B. HORNICK, GLADYS M. ELLIOTT, ORA IVERSON.

THE TIGER has received excellent support from its staff. Such support we believe, throughout the year, will enable the present management to equal if not surpass the high standard set by the preceding Tiger officials.

We wish to thank every member of the staff for the aid and support given us in getting out our first issue. The Faculty have helped us out of many difficulties, and we also wish to thank them, especially Miss Southwick, Miss Otto and Miss Menzel.

The Fall athletic season is now in full sway, but the captains and managers continually appeal for more candidates with little result. For instance, a man decides to try out for track and appears for training and coaching with the rest of the track men. Immediately he finds, much to his surprise, that the other fellows usually beat him in his event. After training faithfully for several weeks, the big team is practically picked and receives the greater part of the coach's attention. In most cases the boy not on the team gives up in disgust and tries some other sport next season. Thus with no one specializing in one branch of athletics, a time comes when the school is without veteran athletes about which to build its team.

This fault can be remedied by the class team captains. The school teams get trips and outside meets, as well as representing the school in the League meets, with an opportunity of winning the coveted Block L, but the unsuccessful candidates have no incentive to work, and consequently they quit, believing strongly that they are incapable of ever being successful athletes.

Class team captains and managers, it's up to you. Make your activity attractive to the athletes unable to place on the school teams. Get dual meets and matches with other class teams—give everybody a chance, and now and then a word of encouragement or praise quietly spoken will do a world of good. When once you get a fellow interested in your branch of athletics, keep him interested and the standard of the school teams of the future will be greatly raised.

The organization of an orchestra has been tried several times, but due to lack of support, these attempts have proved failures. However, as this paper goes to press a new movement is started by Willard Beattie, '10, with the support of several seniors and numerous under-classmen. The plans if given the proper support should be successful.

A school orchestra, besides being a source of enjoyment for its members, would entertain the student-body at large by furnishing music at the rallies and various student-body meetings. Such an orchestra would be a popular organization in this school, and THE TIGER takes this opportunity to ask the students to support Mr. Beattie in making the orchestra a success.

The football season is at hand and the team will need the support of every one. Since the fire the games have been played across the Bay on the Alameda Recreation Grounds. These grounds are inconvenient to reach and many do not go to the games on this account.

Fellows, our team is light and nearly all of the players are new material; so stand the inconvenience and go to all the games, for without support no team can win a championship. If the games are played in Alameda bring your "shouting voice" and root for your team. You do your best to attend the games and they will certainly do their best to win for the school.

Keep your Tiger handy and when you start out on a shopping tour glance over the ads, then buy of our advertisers. Show that the school appreciates the dealers' support of the paper by mentioning THE TIGER. This causes you little trouble and enables us to secure the advertiser for the next issue.

It affords us great pleasure, upon our return to school, to greet our old friends of the exchange column, but there are many familiar faces missing. In the future, we would like to recognize more of our old friends, as well as make acquaintance with a great many new ones.

The worst fault we encounter with our exchanges is in arrangement, several having advertisements in the front pages of the issue. While it may be said that "ads print the paper" just as "money makes the mare go," it is our honest opinion that nothing cheapens the appearance of a paper more than the placing of ads in the front pages, and it is scarcely fair to those whose ads appear in the back of the issue. But we are glad to say that the foregoing does not apply to many of our exchanges, and hope that this fault will not appear again in issues which are otherwise exceedingly good.

"Crimson and White," New York State Normal High School, Albany.—You could use many more cuts without detriment to the appearance of your paper. Also, the different departments should be kept separate. It is these little things that make the appearance of a paper all that it should be.

"Cogswell," San Francisco.—Your commencement issue was a distinct success, "Cogswell." The stories, cuts and photographs, all combined, made it the best issue of its size among our exchanges.

"Herald," Atlantic City.—Your cover is not up to standard of other high school papers. If the ads which appear in front were in the back, your issue would be greatly improved.

"Hitchcock Sentinel," San Rafael.—Have received several of your entertaining little papers as well as your commencement issue. We think that an index would add greatly to the convenience of your commencement issues. Also, do more than recognize your exchanges. Your paper was otherwise very good.

"Joshua Palm," Goldfield High School.—Considering the fact that this is your first appearance as a school paper, you have done fairly well. You could, however, arrange your issue better by the use of cuts for the different departments and the placing of all your ads in the back of the paper.

"Manzanita," Watsonville High School.—Yours is indeed a good paper in proportion to the size of your school. The different departments are clearly defined and the arrangement is good. Why not use more cuts?

"Red and White," Lakeview High School, Chicago.—Your paper was interesting from cover to cover, all the articles being interesting and the arrangement good. But, with a school of your size, do you not think you could make a larger issue for commencement?

Your "Freshman Number" gave us many good laughs, Chapparel. Come again, you're always welcome.

"Russ," San Diego.—We think that a better place for the "Russ" staff could be found than on the first page of the paper-and that another good story would add decidedly to your issue.

"Sequoia," Redwood City.—Your paper is good, the only thing lacking being the exchange column. Why discontinue it?

"Tamalpais Graduate."—You have done exceedingly well, and have certainly made a success of your paper, with such a small graduating class. Your stories, though short, are good.

"Tocsin," Santa Clara High School.—Yours was one of our best exchanges, "Tocsin." Your cover design was unsurpassed, and throughout the entire paper there was not one thing to criticize. Your stories are all good and cuts are used to great advantage.

"The Far Darter," St. Helena.—Your joshes under the heading of "Medicine for Wrinkles" are clever. Your stories are good and the pictures add decidedly to the appearance of the paper.

"The Totem," Juneau High School.—Your stories and articles afforded us great pleasure and gave us an insight into Alaskan manners and customs among the natives. You should devote more space to school-notes and keep your ads in the back of the issue.

As we go to press, we would like to acknowledge the receipt of the following issues, which came too late for criticism:

"The Mistletoe," Willits Union High School.

"The Review," Sacramento High School.

"The Lowell," Lowell High School.

"Green and Gold," Tuolumne County High, Sonora.

Ode to James Lick

O. C. CAMPBELL, '10

Here's to the school that so fondly we love,
    The school that has made us its own;
And though far away from it we may rove,
    To wander 'mid strangers alone,
Our hearts will e'er remember the past
    And brighten with memories quick,
When backward our glances we cast
    And think of our school days at Lick.

A blessing be e'er on those who hold
    Lick's trust in charge, with love so deep,
And may our colors, black and gold,
    His sacred memory green e'er keep—
A blessing that in joy and truth
    Will crown his name with laurels thick,
That gives not only Lick to youth,
    But endless youth to Lick.

FIRST RALLY.

On August 18, 1909, the first rally of the new school year was held. Over the windows were hung the Lick emblem and yellow drapery. Things were in a commotion, for the Lick spirit was high; even the Freshmen were inspired with the realization that they too belonged to "Dear Old Lick."

The four classes took their new rally quarters with promptness and order as though it was the middle of the year. The new Senior Class, '10, filled well the stairs that have been presided over by our former Seniors.

A quietness spread over the whole assemblage for a second, then, as President Pitchford stepped forward, he was greeted with three rousing cheers under Al Wetmore's leadership. President Pitchford asked for a few words from Mr. Merrill, who was accorded a rousing welcome on his appearance. Mr. Merrill spoke on school government and a few important points to have in view the coming year. Then he spoke of the creditable way in which the first rally had been assembled.

President Pitchford next introduced our new yell leader, Al Wetmore, who gave a short talk especially to the "Scrubs" on getting a yell-book. Captain Bell spoke a few words on the importance of turning out early for track and of the unusual opportunities for new men to make the team.

We should have been very surprised to have seen our acting Captain Smith talk to us on football when he was called, but owing to his absence, "Shark" Thornton gave a few words on football. Captain Margo of the swimming team boosted the aquatic sport so that it impressed everyone. Here also fine opportunities were shown for an energetic athlete to win swimming honors.

Our "Tiger" was boosted up by Editor Chatfield; a reminder to look out for jokes, especially new ones, was given us and for any other news that would improve "The Tiger." Manager White gave us a talk on "Tiger" finances and showed how welcome all ads were. He also spoke of the importance of trading with our advertisers and of getting a "Tiger" subscription right away.

Mr. Chilcote spoke of the merits of the "Debating Society" and was hopeful of its increase in membership which will bring it up as one or the largest society in the "Debating League" of California."

By this time the meeting was well along. Al Wetmore proved his worth as yell leader and won the admiration of the "rooting section" by the "classy" motions and gesticulations he went through. After one of those tremendously enthusiastic "Ali—Bi—Bo" and a "Brakety—Ax," which re-echoed across the corridors with a deafening noise, President Pitchford adjourned the meeting.

We all felt that our officers were going to lead us through a most successful year in all our activities.

SECOND RALLY.

Our second rally, called to order on September first, was of great importance, the main topic being the discussion of the merits and faults of the Academic Athletic League. A "Brakety—Ax" was followed with a discussion by H. Henderson on a few points concerning the A. A. L. He brought up the poor manner in which the basketball championship was managed between Oakland and Wilmerding and also asked for an explanation of the financial situation and how the money is expended that is taken in at all of the final games.

Mr. Merrill then spoke on the general athletic situation of the present time. He put plainly before us the difficulties that have arisen in the schools as well as in the league. He said in part that about three years ago there was over a thousand dollars in the treasury of the A. A. L., and owing to the present dwindled state of the treasury, it shows that there has been some sort of mismanagement. That the blue-blank system is not quite as efficient as it should be, was another point brought out by Mr. Merrill. When one boy from another school could be signed up on penmanship and rhetoric to play a game against boys of other schools who are forced to reach a high standard in subjects that require conscientious work and hard study, proves that the blue-blank system is not as perfect as it might be. In concluding he said that his understanding was that the Academic Athletic League had established a new constitution to correct, as far as possible, errors made in the past and he expressed his wish that it would be a success.

Thornton then asked for an explanation of the awarding of gold footballs to teams which tie for a championship.

In order to throw a little more light on the unsettled condition of affairs, President Cloud of the A. A. L. consented to attend the rally. He was the next speaker and in explaining the points brought out by the previous speakers said that the greatest fault due to the low condition in the treasury was the loss incurred by the issue of a handbook containing information regarding the A. A. L. and also in the last basketball season. As far as blue-blanks were concerned he said that after years of effort on the part of those interested in the League this was the best system for a scholarship standing for competition that they could attain and that as yet, no other better one had been suggested. He furthermore explained the change the league had made in the constitution, telling of the new Sub-Leagues of the A. A. L., to which every school sends two delegates, one of whom must be a student and the other a graduate or a faculty member of the school. There are certain geographical divisions of the State which form these sub-leagues. After they have settled the sub-league games, each sub-league competes for the semifinals, the winners of which play the final game.

Mr. Cloud was willing to answer any questions concerning the A. A. L. to the best of his ability, but there was no further discussion on his part.

Mr. Tibbetts, Secretary of the A. A. L., spoke of the point of view that many of the boys take in regards to medals, saying that there is too much of a tendency of working toward a medal of pure gold than for working for the glory and pleasure that is connected with athletics.

Manager White and Editor Chatfield ended the meeting with short addresses on the school paper.

After an old time "Ali—Bi—Bo" President Pitchford closed the second very successful rally.

RECORD BOOK.

The "Record Book" has not received any new material as yet this year, owing to the finishing up of some work in it by its former custodian, Willard Beatty. However, we know it will progress rapidly when it is turned over to Miss Fraser, its future owner, as we know what Miss Fraser can do, and have great faith in her ability.

CAMERA CLUB.

The first important business of the Camera Club this year was to elect a new President and Treasurer. Mr. Hornick, elected President last term, found it necessary to resign and Mr. Creighton, former Treasurer, left school. At a special meeting of the club, held on August 20th Mr. Hill and Mr. Sullivan were elected to the respective positions of President and Treasurer.

Any student is eligible to become a member of the Camera Club. The dues are fifteen cents a month, and this entitles every member to all of the privileges of the club, including a well-equipped dark-room.

Much pleasure is derived from the work in the club and many enjoyable outings are indulged in by its members.

"LICK DEBATING SOCIETY."

The Lick Debating Society is once more in full sway. Mr. Chilcote, the new President, seems to have inspired many of the students with the importance of the society, as seen by the large attendance at its meetings. At the first meeting, held on August 25th, Mr. Chilcote enumerated all of the society's attractions and a large number of Freshmen have applied for membership, in spite of the amount of ten cents a month required from every member.

The Senate, Dramatic, Technical and Literary departments have all been reorganized, and give the members of the society a chance to specialize in any one department if they choose to. The first meeting of the Senate was largely attended and several warm discussions ensued on "airships," and "woman suffrage." This department brings into evidence the extemporaneous debaters. Under Mr. Chilcote, the Senate is becoming a popular place to discuss the more important questions of the day.

Mr. Hills, chairman of the Dramatic Department, has some ideas up his sleeve which may be presented to us in the form of playlets, sometime before Christmas.

The Technical Department is in charge of very capable hands, those of Mr. McNair.

The Literary Department, under Mr. Hirschler's skill, is at present working up a mock trial, to be given before the society some time in the near future.

To Mr. Carlson, chairman of the Interclass Debating League, much credit is due. Interclass debating this year has been run off with no trouble whatever, and already each class has picked its team. The teams to represent the classes are:

Freshmen—Mr. Boruch, Mr. Cody, Mr. Eastman; alternate, Mr. Snooks.
Sophomore—Miss Boyle, Miss Simons, Mr. Worth; alternate, Mr. Lenzen.
Junior—Mr. Hills, Mr. McNair, Mr. Hirschler; alternate, Mr. Klein.
Senior—Mr. Oehlman, Mr. Montgomery, Miss Iverson; alternate, ———.

The winning class team will be given the custody of the Lincoln Bust, on whose plate its class numerals will be inscribed.

By the time this "Tiger" is issued the three most successful debaters of the class teams will have made the final school team, which is scheduled to debate the Berkeley Ecclesia. There is no reason why Lick should not win this debate, with such promising material to try out for the team. After good, hard work on the part of the team we hope that their efforts may be rewarded by success.

"THE THIRTEEN CLASS."

No longer can we look upon 1912 as Freshmen. They have left their place for 1913 to occupy, and we here take the opportunity of giving you our heartiest welcome, "Thirteen." You have started out with the proper spirit and if it continues you may be sure of a successful career in this school.

At the girls' rally the Thirteen Class was well represented by speakers, among whom were the Misses Todd, McLaughlin, McKibben, M. Brown, Hauerken and Kern. The interest taken by the boys, also, in athletics has been marked for a Freshman class.

A picnic is being planned for the Thirteen Class by 1911, to be given on the tenth of September down the Ocean Shore Railroad.

At a special class meeting of the Eleven Class, held on September 3rd, all of the Freshmen were urgently invited to attend the picnic, as it provided a fine chance for them to get acquainted with each other. Miss Otto assured the Freshmen that there was positively no danger, not even in the tunnel that unfortunately had to be passed through. Miss Southwick suggested a very informal way of getting acquainted would be to have everyone wear a tag with his or her name on it. The two classes greeted this as a fine suggestion and it remains to be seen if everyone will carry out this plan. The Freshmen were assured the best kind of a time at the picnic, provided the weather was all right.

Under the decision of the Faculty, the Thirteen Class will not be organized under the old plan for at least the first quarter. An advisory committee, consisting of Miss Otto, Miss Adams and Mr. Heymann, have chosen temporarily, for officers of the '13 Class the following:

Mr. Deleray of the Senior Class, President; Mr. Chilcote of the Junior Class, Vice-President; Miss Boyle of the 2nd Year Class, Secretary.

Under these capable hands, "Thirteen," you may be sure of getting a good start.

Alumni

Heretofore news of Lick graduates not attending college has been very hard to obtain. However, we have succeeded in getting some bits of information that will be interesting to many.

The midgets of the '06 Class, A. Currie and "Billie" Marcus, are making names for themselves. In nearly every Sunday newspaper the name of W. Marcus is seen as the winner of a tennis tournament. "Bill" is employed in the Metropolis Bank. Currie is a head man in one of the Santa Fe surveying gangs.

Earl Lieb, the famous end of '07, is a full-fledged contractor.

In the S. P. drafting shop in the Flood Building are several Lick men. Fred Block, '08, graces one table, Sweezey, '05, is at another, as are also Newton, '08, and Mont Johnson, '06.

Frank Brown, '07, is trying to help Jimmie Wise increase the capacity of the Gas Company.

"Dutch" Holmes, '06, is at present employed in Portland as a constructing engineer. He is to be married shortly to Edith Sells, ex-'08.

Fred Irving, '05, is helping his father sell paint at the Paraffine Paint Company.

Helene Blackwell, '04, is married and lives in Ukiah.

Mrs. Harry Euler (nee Clara Dillon, '04), has a brand new daughter.

We were surprised and pleased to hear of the engagement of Bertha Williams, '06, to Ed Seegal. The marriage will take place next spring.

"Billie" Henderson, the popular Gas man of the '06 Class, married Sadie Flack, '04, last June. Thus was the end of an old schoolroom romance.

Seminario, halfback of the champion '05 team, is at present residing in Berkeley after a long sojourn at his plantation in Ecuador.

Bert Golcher, '04, is the proud possessor of a six months' old baby.

Eddie Dietz is also ditto.

Joe Hill, '05, is manager of the California Fruit Canneries.

Frank MacDonald, '07, is in the dairy-produce business for himself.

Paul Miller, '08, is at present clerk in the Rex Hotel.

L. P. Stellar, '03, holds a position with the Forderer Cornice Works.

Hirshfeld, '07, is working in Napa for the Napa Lumber Company.

Robert Gardiner, '09, is at present working for his father in the real estate business in this city.

"Chick" O'Connor, '05, is in the city at present and has been helping Sid Holman coach the football team.

CALIFORNIA.

It seems peculiar to be writing to the whole Lick school, about certain members who happen to be gathered at the University of California to pursue their studies, but as this certain bunch has stuck together pretty well, it is not so hard. The '09 bunch over there has a peculiar distinction: Thirteen '09ers entered the Class of '13 at college, on Friday the 13th; filed their study-cards on the 23rd; and one of their number, Leland Weber to be exact, is number 13 in the 13th Company of the U. C. Cadets! How's that for going some?

In addition to the '09ers entering this term, enough members of other classes are entering to swell the number of Lick freshmen at college to twenty! Of this number, Elna Clifford is the only girl, and it looks pretty good when you meet her on the campus.

Hugh Webster is the youngest of us, as regards class standing at Lick, being an '11 man, who has gumption enough to take a "special" course at college. Next in line in Rolla Watt, the "Kow Kollege Kid," who passed the entrance exs, and is entered regularly in the College of Agriculture (snap course).

Among the illustrious ones who are entered this year, stands "Vic" Lenzen, who all Lick men will be interested to know, has become quite a "rough-neck," even deigning to participate in "that rough game" called push-ball!

Rosenwald, Wills, Small, Beatty, Dickey (who is to become a chemist!), DeLano, Jones, Hunt and Strouss are a few more, and Gay, '07, and Bloch, Cortelyou, Larzelere and Howeisner, '08, are entered in the lucky class of '13.

Hammond, DeLano, Dickey, Howeisner and Hunt have been the "fall guys" for the amusement of the "Sophs." so far, and were forced to march up and down in front of North Hall with their pants rolled up, their coats on inside-out, and sucking milk bottles. It is rumored that Lenzen was caught, but according to his story, he was released before being subjected to any indignities. I have my doubts about the latter—but believe it if you want to. The story is also going the rounds that Dick Jones has learned how to blow ten bubbles in a bath-tub full of cold water, and has to get up before breakfast every morning and mow the lawn. Wills and Rosenwald are living in a house, supposed to be immune to "Sophs."; nevertheless, they were awakened late one night, and marched to the bath room. Wills was sensible, and took his. medicine like a man—he was only tubbed three times. Rosenwald felt himself a match for any number of Sophomores (derived from Greek, "wise-fool"), and consequently it took eight immersions to calm him down. As a reward for his bravery, he was forced to chew a piece of soap, and ended by amusing his captors by pulling the plug out of the tub of water with his teeth.

Of the upper classmen, "Bones" Eveleth, Gallagher, Arnold Brown, Jaenicke, Tinning, Peterson, Kennedy (Irish), Czarnecke, and a few others are among the Sophs., while "String-bean" Barrieau's cheerful face, along with "Ike" Doane and "Brick" White, is further along in wisdom.

"Yank" Rodgers is out for a semester, but will return to California at the end of that time.

Two of the '09 girls, Miss Frank and Miss Winter, have entered the S. F. Normal with the avowed intention of becoming "old maid schoolma'ams." Clare Hodges is intending to enter San Jose Normal.

Felt and Little are working in Virginia City, Nevada. The former claims to be 2100 feet under ground, and is trying to earn enough money to enter college next year.

McKeehan and Lawton are laboring at different jobs with the same intention. Bill Ashley is taking a six months' course at Poly to make up a few more units necessary to enter college, and Bert Banta and Sahlbach are doing the same at Berkeley High. Freeman Smith is helping Kellogg with the Lick exhibit at the Seattle Exposition, and has spoken of his intention of entering a medical college. Alvin Stern is back in San Francisco—for what reason, no one knows. Bertha Knell, Lillian Capp and Ingaborg Lindstrom are living lives of leisure—at present.

This covers nearly every one of whom I know—some may not have been given the notoriety they desire, but it is not my fault. Anyone who has done anything particularly foolish (or brilliant) has been given special mention, and when the others do the same, they may expect headlines too!

STANFORD.

The enrollment of Lick students at Stanford differs little from last semester.

Dave Walker, '05, is back taking graduate work, as is also Ed Rogers, '05. Harriet Park, '06, has again majored in art and her brother Carl, '06, after a year's absence has returned to pursue his studies in engineering.

The '08 Class last year sent more men to Stanford than any of its predecessors and most of them have again registered.

Howard Dietterle, '08, and Robert Clyde, '08, both members of last year's Freshman crew, have returned. Clyde is a member of the Kappa Alpha fraternity and Dietterle is an Encina man, eating at the "Breakers."

"Ted" Everett, '08, a member of the Phi Gamma Delta fraternity, is out for football.

Ashleigh Simpson, '09, is the Stanford correspondent for the San Francisco Call. He is a member of the Sigma Alpha Epsilon fraternity.

"King Dodo" Barnett did not return this fall, but expects to work a semester and return in January.

Leon Vanatta, '06, is working with his father in the electrical business and will not return to college.

Cecil Stocker Simon, '09, is the only new arrival this year from Lick. His anxiety to participate in the Sophomore-Freshman rush was his first offense and his eagerness to obtain "Tiger" news his second. Otherwise his start has been most promising.

MECHANICAL DRAWING.

Mr. Heymann has the "Unlucky 13ers" down to steady work, and they are struggling along on the fourth sheet, hoping by the end of the quarter to have mastered the art of lettering.

Most of the Second Year students have finished the second sheet of orthographic projections; while the Junior apprentices are working hard on their riveting and cross-section sheets, thereby receiving the foundation for more complicated work.

The Seniors, Johnson, Thornton and Lind, are drawing the details of a steam turbine; the patterns and castings, as well as the machining of which, is to be done in the various shops just as soon as completed.

Spring is drawing a one-cylinder gas engine to be used in the school, and "Dutch" Reimer is working on general constructions.

Bell is the only apprentice of whom it might be said he is doing outside work. "Ham" is making a set of drawings of a yacht, which when finished he expects to have built.

PATTERN SHOP.

The Freshmen are well started with their various joints, having received lectures from Mr. McLeran on general conduct and on the manipulation of their tools.

Mr. McLeran has endeavored to break the habit of old students of calling him "Mac," but his all-too-wise apprentices seem to persist in addressing him with the familiar salutation. Don't forget there's a graduation day, fellows.

The Junior apprentices have done many odd jobs, among which are a complete set of drawings and patterns for a special vise to be used exclusively in the shop, it having a much stronger grip than the ones now in use.

The Seniors have started in the new term with renewed energy, and if they finish as strongly as they have started, they will have a thorough knowledge of pattern-making.

Uhte, according to Mr. McLeran, is now foreman of the shop; "Dutch's" main lookout being to warn the Freshmen against the using of the band-saw and also to keep account of what work is being done. He is finishing a four-cylinder gasoline engine for Bruns.

Von der Mehden is now doing outside work, having completed a set of drawings of the crank case for an opposed-cylinder gas engine.

Sparrowe has attained that nicety of skill in the use of his tools that comes with much practice; however, his personal modesty prevents us commenting further on his work.

FORGE SHOP.

Down in the blacksmith shop an exceedingly large class of second-year boys have been gazing upon the steam-hammer with awe, and have been accumulating a plentiful supply of blisters from pounding upon cold iron.

They have been instructed as to the different parts of a forge and have been initiated into the mystery of fire-building and almost all of them can now make very creditable fires.

They are now engaged in the first exercises and are rapidly learning the use of their tools under the able instruction of Mr. Mathis. He is very much pleased with the spirit of the young blacksmiths and expects some excellent work from them before the term is over. No repairing work has come into the shop as yet, but Mr. Mathis expects to have some before long so that the students can get practical experience.

At the Seattle Fair Mr. Mathis observed the work of some Igorrote blacksmiths with great attention. They are natives of the Philippine Islands, and, although they have been using their tools for hundreds of years, Mr. Mathis thinks that some of his tools, at least, are better than theirs, and hopes that the boys make as good use of them as the natives do of their crude ones.

FOUNDRY.

In the foundry Mr. Lacoste has a large class of beginners engaged in making the easier exercises. They have poured once already, most of the molds being the blocks for the machine shop and the first exercise. They will now proceed with the more difficult molds. He has also poured three gas engines, two of which came out all right. In a short time he expects to make a gas engine of about 5 horse-power for the machine shop apprentices to work upon. No large jobs have presented themselves as yet, but we expect to have some before the term is over.

MACHINE SHOP.

The machinists are doing very creditable work for so early in the year. The Juniors are finishing up their chipping-block exercise, learning the intricacies of the drilling machine and center gouge, although a few laggards are still at their chipping, having knocked their knuckles more times than they have hit their chisels. Those who are taking the apprenticeship course are well on to the second and third exercises, and very soon will be doing their lathe work.

"Chief" Dixon, who considers himself assistant instructor to Mr. Sunkel, roams about the shop giving advice to the unwary. Beware! Juniors, or he will fix you when he gets you on the engine.

The Seniors are working on various jobs. Dow is finishing a 4½x2½x4 boiler-feed pump, which is to be used in the boiler-room instead of the steam injector.

Chapman and King are putting together a 9x4 steam hoist, and Gilliland among other jobs has made an electro-magnet which is to be used in the chemistry laboratory.

Smith is now a graduate vise-mender, and he hasn't any hard feelings toward the "Scrubs" because of their unsolicited aid in his "course" (?).

Pratt spends most of his time instructing aspiring engineers and doing odd jobs.

CHEMISTRY

In the chemistry laboratory the work is progressing nicely under the supervision of Mr. Tibbetts. The classes in general chemistry are much smaller than in the past, but Mr. Tibbetts reports that there is some good material among them. He hopes that they will soon learn to handle their apparatus and experiments in a capable manner.

The junior apprentices are engaged in preliminary work upon a system of qualitative analysis. This system has been worked out in the research laboratory of the Massachusetts Institute of Technology and is unquestionably the best system worked out up-to-date. This system, helped out by some original ideas of Mr. Tibbetts, is furnishing them some very interesting work.

The seniors are now analyzing some of the alloys, principally brass and babbitt. They are using the most rapid modern methods for commercial purposes.

Of last year's class two have secured positions in their chosen profession. Marshal is an assistant analyst in the soil department of the Alvarado Beet Sugar Refinery, and Boxton is working for a chemical company in Sacramento. Bates is with the Southern Pacific. "Dutch" Merkelbach has returned to school to finish his course.

COOKING.

Due to Miss Hyde's efforts, and also to the ambition of the cooking classes, some very praiseworthy results have been obtained by the girls.

Evidently there is a growing demand for good cooks, as the cooking department now boasts of a morning and an afternoon class. The morning section devotes some time to preparing luncheons for the faculty table, and their ability has been most skillfully shown in this work.

In addition to this, both classes have made numerous appetizing dishes, such as apple jelly, grape jelly and plum jam. They have also pickled watermelon rind, and canned peaches and pears.

SEWING.

The Freshmen are working diligently upon the practice pieces for their sample books, which they will have completed by the end of the quarter. They are very anxious to begin the white work, which will no doubt appeal to them greatly, as it has to the Freshmen classes of previous years. In connection with the work in the practice books, they are kept quite busy making aprons for the woodwork and chemistry departments.

The second year girls are employed for the present in taking measures, studying the advantages afforded by the use of the MacDowell System, drafting their own patterns, and making the model waist. This class is also doing extra work in making blouses for the woodwork department.

There is a larger Junior sewing class this year than usual. The girls have been working very conscientiously and many dainty specimens of handsewing have already been completed.

Last, but not least, are the Seniors. They have drafted patterns and are making rapid progress in their tailor sewing. Miss Schomaker and Miss R. Mitchell have begun the model tailor suit, and their work deserves much credit.

Each of the four classes is showing an undivided interest in its work, and therefore we may duly expect some good results from the Sewing Room in the future.

The American Football Association

Since the old game of American football has been abolished in two of the prominent universities and also in some of the high schools, it has been felt by some of our public-spirited citizens who take an active interest in boys' athletics, that the boys had not been getting the best results from the game. For this reason they have formed an Association whereby they can better the present conditions.

In the first place, the Association stands for true sportsmanship and everything that tends to produce friendship and manliness among the boys in athletics. The fact that such men as Wm. Reid of Belmont and Wm. and Geo. Middleton, whom we all know as straightforward and sportsmanlike men, are prime factors in this Association, proves to you that the organization will be the greatest help that a school could have along athletic lines. They have taken steps to secure competent officials for games and also provide for coaches for the high schools. They do not intend to run off a schedule of games, but will make arrangements for games for the schools desiring them. It is also their object to see that these games are carried on as they should be. In other words, their object is to boost for what is right in athletics.

Delegates to Leagues

At the beginning of each school year, delegates are elected by the Board of Control to the three Leagues under whose auspices our athletic teams compete. These representatives are supposed to make arrangements for League games, provide for new rules and regulations governing the different sports, and report to the Board of Control the proceedings of the meetings of the League which they are representing.

Charles Mel, '06, and H. A. Sexton, '11, were elected delegates to the Academic League for the coming year. Herrman Henderson, '10, is our delegate to the Bay Counties League, and Al Margo, '10, represents us in the San Francisco Athletic League.

Charles Mel has been elected President of the A. A. L. Sub-League and Al. Margo has been chosen as Secretary for the San Francisco Athletic League for the coming year.

Mr. Mel, as President of the San Francisco Sub-League, is unable to serve as a delegate from Lick, and Jerome Barjean has been elected graduate delegate to the Sub-League.

Our Coaches

It is a well-known fact that athletics as practised by the high schools not only tend to develop a boy physically but also morally. However, the latter development depends greatly on the manner in which he is taught and brought up to realize what true sportsmanship is. To treat the other fellow as fairly and squarely as you would want him to treat you, to never lose control of your temper, and to play as clean a game as ever could be played, are a few of the points to keep in mind always.

This sort of feeling is being so thoroughly instilled in all of the boys out for football that we find, although they are not a heavy, husky bunch, they can put up as good a game as any of them. It is to William and George Middleton that the credit falls for this condition of affairs in our school.

Through their hard work and personal character, they have established a feeling of true sportsmanship among the boys that any school could be proud of. All this has been done in time that was most valuable to them and which could have been spent in other lines, but still they saw where they were able to be of assistance to the boys of the school. Although they will not be able to come and coach us as often as they would like to do for the coming season, they are going to give us as much of their spare time as possible.

However, we have a man who has been brought up along athletic lines by the Middleton brothers, and who was our football captain in 1909, acting as coach for the coming season. This man is Sidney Holman. He is going to put that spirit into the fellows that Bill and George were so successful in doing.

Football

Once more the padded pants and jerseys are scurrying around the yard, and the oldest known heavier-than-air flying machine is sailing through the air to the resounding whack of the cleated foot. Only five of last year's squad are back at school, two of whom played throughout the league games.

They are: E. Smith, end; Thornton, guard; Bliss, sub-center; Bell, sub-guard, and H. Henderson, sub-halfback.

At the annual football banquet last fall, Jimmie Holt was elected to captain this year's team, but much to his disappointment he was unable to attend school this term. So at a special meeting, Ernest Smith was elected temporary captain. At the same time candidates for the team were called for. The call was readily responded to and a large squad has practised every night. It will be a very difficult problem to make a new team, but the boys are in earnest, and that looks promising.

Sid Holman, who was our star halfback and captain last year, will be active coach. Will and George Middleton will be in charge, but on account of pressing business will not be able to help us all the time, so Holman very kindly consented to do the active coaching. All those who remember his brilliant playing last year, as well as the able manner in which he captained the team, will rest assured that he will turn out a fine team.

The back field will be entirely new, and this will be the hardest part of the team to build up. Holman, Holt, Wittenmeyer, Padilla, Murray and Jones have all left, and their shoes will be hard to fill. "Crumby" Thornton, H. Henderson, "Dutch" Reimer, Nash, "Ham" Bell, Rust, Wynne and Winter are trying for the back field positions this year.

The line will be hard to substitute also, but by the looks of the boys striving for the line positions there will be a hard tussle for places.

Bliss will find it hard to offset those trying for center, and even temporary Captain Smith will have to work hard to keep his position because of the large number trying out for the end positions.

The decision of our old rival, Lowell, and of Mission High School to play Rugby will decrease the number of games in the Sub-league. Cogswell has entered a football team this year for the first time since joining the A. A. L.

Polytechnic has a veteran team and will make a hard fight for the Sub-league championship.

The Wilmerding team has been left in much the same condition as our team, and it remains to be seen what they will be able to accomplish with their new material.

This lack of experienced players is due for the most part to the fact that the under-classmen leave the support of the football team to the upper-classmen. Thus graduation makes vacancies that are extremely hard to fill. Under-classmen, Freshmen and Sophomores, it's up to you to come out and try out for the team. There should be little complaint, for the boys will fight hard when the time comes; however, they will need the support of every member of the student body.

Track

The track season started with an enthusiastic meeting at which about thirty boys showed their intention of donning spiked shoes and trying for a place on the school team. Noticeable among them were some Freshmen. We depend on these Freshmen for our future track teams and hope to see many more before the season ends. This is a sport in which size does not count, but needs steady training to make a successful runner. Some are naturally speedy and show it in their Freshman year, but it takes others until their Senior year to be successful. The latter really gain more glory than the former, by their long, persistent work. Therefore if you don't run fast enough at first, try till you are fast! All boys have speed in them but it needs development to bring results.

The veterans from last year's squad are Captain "Ham" Dell and Wallace in the distance events, Dickson, Tooker, Corker, Mgr., Maynard in the sprints, and Hohman in the weight events. Among the promising new runners are Rogers, '13, and Clark, '11, in the sprints; McFarland, '12, McCrea, '11, and "Mascot" Nixon, '13, in the weights; House, '11, and Dunshee, '11, in the high jump and pole vault. This will not be enough to select a team of fifteen to represent us in the field days and we need more candidates.

Don't look at the present alone but also to the future. Start your career on the track now and make it a successful one for yourself as well as the school.

Basketball

The basketball season has not yet started, but will begin late this fall when the interclass games are finished. From the class teams the best players will be picked to form a good squad to start the spring practice.

The players from last year are Captain Sparrowe, Westphal, Bert Woods, McHenry and Wood. Around these will be developed a team that ought to fight hard for the championship. Dick Creighton was elected captain, but was unable to be with us this year, and Sparrowe has been elected in his place. Practice games with club and high school teams will be arranged and the prospects for a good team are very bright.

Swimming .

The swimming season is now well on its way. An enthusiastic meeting was held early in the season and a large number of candidates signed up for the team. The veterans of last year who are still at school are Capt. Margo, our crack quarter and half miler; Paul, 220 yds.; Dreyer, 100 yds., and Steele. The fellows have been training hard at Sutro Baths and the Presidio Life Saving Station. A number of dual meets have been arranged with schools around the bay so that the fellows will gain experience that will later be invaluable to them.

Since the B. C. L. has taken up swimming the school will enter a team in their meets. The A. A. L. will take place early in November. From the present outlook, we shall have a most successful season.

The Inter-Class League

The founding of the Inter-Class League dates back to the year 1907, when the class 1907 were seniors. Its fundamental purpose was to increase the interest of the students along athletic lines and also to develop the younger material of the school for the big teams of the future. It has aroused much interest in the past, as was shown by the many hotly contested track and different field events held since its formation. The League gives opportunity for every boy or girl to take part in athletics in the school, as any member of the Student Body is eligible to compete for his or her class team. Each sport is managed by a separate committee appointed by the President of the Student Body. However, if there are any who wish to compete in the interclass meets they should look up their class captain or manager for the sport in which they intend to compete and let him know what they intend doing in athletics. He in turn will see that your name is handed to the committee who will enter your name for competition.

The League affords every student in the school a chance to fight for his class and also to show his school spirit by taking an active interest in student activities. It is up to the class Presidents to arouse this spirit in their organizations and it is hoped that keen interest will be taken along the line of interclass activities for this and the coming seasons. The sports to be managed by the Interclass League for the present term are: football, track, basketball, swimming and tennis.

Football.

In looking over the games of last year, we see the class of '09 the victors, having won the final game from 1910. From the present outlook it is hard to name the victors for the coming year on account of the situation of the big school team. They require almost entirely new material and therefore have to select the players from the class teams. Thus it can readily be seen that the interclass will also need new material. Consequently it is necessary for the new·material to come forward as soon as possible. It will be interesting to see which class puts forth the largest amount of men.

Track.

The interclass field-day takes place semi-annually on the Wilmerding track. It is an event in which every fellow ought to take part. Each class has an equal chance of.winning this coming meet as there is not a large number of men training this season. The more men a class puts in the field the better chances it has in winning the meet. Each fellow that comes out and trains means just that much more help towards the victory of his class. The question now comes who is going to win?

Basketball.

The same may be said of basketball as has been said of football. New material is needed in all the classes to take the place of those men who will be required to fill the vacancies on the big team. It rests with each individual to stand by his class and work for the championship.

Swimming.

The interclass swimming tournament was held on Saturday, Sept. 4th, at Sutro Baths. It proved a great success, especially for the Class of 1910. However, there was some promising material to be seen in the lower classes in the races. Captain Margo proved to be the star of the day, having won three events. Some of the races were particularly interesting and close. The 100-yd. and 50-yd. races were especially exciting. Halbert and Maunder were the most conspicuous competitors from the '11 Class, while Rohde was the only '12 Class man to take a place. Captain Margo is looking forward for some good material to develop in the '13 Class. The relay was won rather easily by the '10 Class but was more closely contested for second place between '11 and '12. The results of the tournament were:

50-yd.—1st, Halbert, '11; 2nd, Maunder, '11; 3rd, Deleray, '10·
100-yd.—1st, Dreyer, '10; 2nd, Litchfield, '11; 3rd, Rohrbach, '10·
220-yd.—1st, Margo, '10; 2nd, Paul, '10; 3rd, Steele, '10·
440-yd.—1st, Margo, '10; 2nd, Rohde, '12; 3rd, Heynemann, '11·
880-yd.—1st, Margo, '10; 2nd, Paul, '10; 3rd, Maunder, '11·
Relay—1st, 1910; 2nd, 1911; 3rd, 1912.
Score—1910, 34; 1911, 16; 1912, 4.

Tennis.

Tennis is a sport that has not been developed to a great extent in this school and therefore affords great opportunities for any tennis aspirants to gain the glory of victory for their class. Al Wetmore has full charge of the arrangements for the interclass owing to the small number of tennis players in the school. Come out and arouse interest in this sport, fellows.

Girls' Athletics

A girls' rally was called on Aug. 25 for the purpose of getting the girls in general and the Freshmen in particular interested in athletics. Miss Otto suggested that all the activities be under the supervision of the "Girls' Pastime Club." The officers of the club are to be a president, secretary and a committee for each activity to be taken up, with the following duties:

To arrange for outings, to make a pennant—an artistic poster,—this poster to have a place for a movable date. To attach a slip of paper beneath this poster on which the girls who desire to go on the outings will leave their names; to put this poster up early in the week so the list will be complete by the day of the outing; to provide a chaperon (teacher or parent); to plan to make their outings interesting as well as profitable.

Miss Otto's plans were unanimously approved of by the girls. Miss Southwick and Miss Bridgman also expressed their approval. Nominations were then declared open for the officers of the club. Miss Gillette was unanimously elected president; Miss Iverson was elected secretary of the club.

Besides the sports already established at Lick, handball was suggested. A tramping club was also urged by some of the girls and many seem to be anxious to test their ability as walkers. The girls were all very enthusiastic over the new plans and the Pastime Club appears to be the best organization ever formed among the girls for the purpose of furthering athletics. In order to get started immediately Miss Gillette appointed the following committees:

Boating—Miss Kern, '13; Miss Nicolson, '10; Miss Jann, '10; Miss Kahn, '12.

Swimming—Miss Hauerken, '13; Miss Boye, '10; Miss Schmelz, '11; Miss Von der Meyden, '12.

Tennis—Miss M. Brown, '13; Miss J. Brown, '11; Miss Bettoli, '12.

Handball—Miss Todd, '13; Miss Bettoli, '12.

Basketball—Miss McLaughlin, '13; Miss S. Feldeman, '11; Miss Boyd, '10.

Tramping Club—Miss McKibbin, '13; Miss Kay, '10; Miss M. Northrup, '12.

Glee Club—Miss Gillette, '10; Miss Erlander, '11; Miss Reinhold, '10.

Basketball.

Although there are more branches of girls' athletics this year than ever before, basketball still seems to be one of the favorite sports. The basketball girls were the first to meet and elect a captain for the coming year. Miss Sophie Felderman was unanimously elected and everyone feels that she will be one of the best captains Lick has ever had. Miss Boyd was elected manager by the Board of Control and, together with Miss Felderman, should produce a team which can hold its own against any of the surrounding schools.

Many of the Freshman girls have come out for basketball and will no doubt soon have a good team of their own. The Sophomores and Juniors are also well represented but more of the Senior girls should come out and practice, if not to make a place on the team, for the pleasure of the sport.

Swimming and Boating.

Swimming and boating were both popular last year and we hope their popularity will continue this year. The committees in charge of these sports have agreed to hold their outings on alternate Wednesday afternoons while the good weather lasts. Miss Otto, Miss Menzel and Miss Adams have offered their services as chaperons, and the girls are sure of having many pleasant times.

Tennis.

The actual tennis practice will not begin until after Christmas, although many have expressed their intention of going out for that sport, and Miss Brown has kindly offered her services to any one who wishes to learn the game.

Tramping Club.

This is one of the new features of the Pastime Club and many seem to be interested in it. The committee is planning to take outings quite frequently. Those of the girls who have cameras should take them along and try their skill as photographers. By the time this appears, the club will have had its first outing, which will take place on Sept. 9. Miss Otto and Miss Southwick will act as chaperons. The girls should all come out and get in training in case of another car-strike!

Handball.

This is also a new branch of athletics and interest in it seems to be mostly among the Freshmen. With all of these activities to choose from, each girl should find some branch of athletics to which to devote her spare time and help to keep the Pastime Club on its feet.

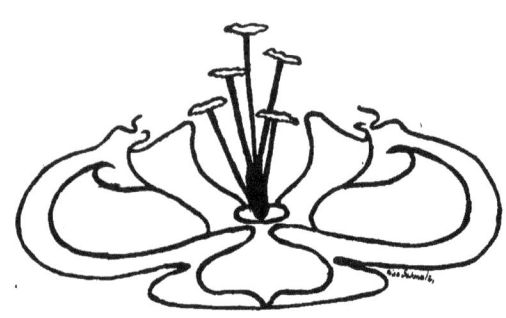

JOSHES

The editor is not responsible for any "personal mention" within this department. If you have any kick coming, write your complaint carefully and legibly on a piece of note-book paper and throw it into the waste basket. [The janitors will probably remove it before you graduate.]

CLASS MEETING

Little Horace, ain't he sweet?
Such a pleasant child to meet;
Not the one to cause vexation,
Never probes in conversation,
Has no questions to harass
The most modest lad or lass,
Tho' he's filled with childish fun
Ever 'tends to number one.
Behaves as nicely as he can,
Quite a perfect little man!

FOILED.

He boiled the water that he
    drank,
By rule he slept and ate,
He wore hygienic overcoats
To get the bulge on fate.
Thus science served him well
And made him microbe proof,
But yesterday he met defeat
By falling off a roof.

Socks and ties should be seen, and not heard.

Windy—Say, Al, is this solution an acid or a base?
Al Wetmore—Huh! Do you take me for a piece of litmus paper?

FAVORITES IN MUSIC.

"Hear Dem Bells".....................................Ends of periods!
"Hush-a-Bye-Baby"..................................The Scrubs
"Keep on Smiling"....................................Al Wetmore
"Dearie" ....Miss Fr-s-r
"Ain't You Coming Back"..............................Padilla
"Bake Dat Chicken Pie"...............................Cooking Class
"Deutschland Uber Alles"..............................T. M. O.
"Two Dark Eyes".....................................Miss M- - - s
"Honey Boy" ....Trainer
"Not Because Your Hair is Curly"......................"Lead"
"Beautiful Eyes" ....Florence
"Everybody Gives Me Good Advice".....................Faculty
"Rocked in the Cradle of the Deep"...................Mechanics
"Rah, Rah, Rah"......................................Wednesday P. M.
"I Got Mine"...Report Cards
"I'm Wise"..Hirschler
"Can't You See I'm Lonely"...........................Campbell
"Just a Gleam of Heaven".............................Basement
"El Capitan" ...."Pitch"
"Always In the Way"..................................The Exes
"All In, Down and Out"...............................After them
    And
"You're Just My Style"...............................C. S. M. A.

There was a young girl called Ruth,
Who, if this tale be the truth,
    Cut off her hair
    To her utter despair,
And that is the tale of poor Ruth!

Is it a man's "funny bone" that laughs up his sleeve for him?

A DREAM?

Last night as I lay asleeping,
I had an awful dream;
Toward me a monster came leaping,
I awakened with a scream!
'Twas a dream, an awful dream.

In one hand it held a pencil,
In the other a yellow book,
I shrank as I gazed upon it
For it yelled with a terrible look,
"Pay your dues!"—'Twas no dream.
But a book, and a look,
An awful look!

Farmer Bug—This fellow may have a very fertile brain but it's awful hard to cultivate.

1913—Please take the splinter from under my nail, Barkis?
Barkis—What have you been doing, Freshie?
1913—Scratching my head, sir.

Ambitious Student—Say, Mike, what is drawing?
Winter—Drawing is thinking and making a mark around a think.

In Senior Cookery.

Miss Hyde: "Miss Fraser, what is a colander?"
Miss Fraser: "Why—er—well, a colander is a pan full of holes."
Miss Hyde: "H'm. Evidently, then, there is nothing in it."

There was a young fellow named White,
Who took all the money in sight;
He goes to our dads,
And makes them take ads
For THE TIGER. He's surely all right.

FROM A SONG
THE VILLAGE BELL WAS SLOWLY DINGING · · · ·

There was a young chappie named Rey,
Who'd nothing whatever to say,
He kept so mum
People thought he was dumb!
It's a shame that we lie this way!

Never throw your old shoes, in back alleys; alligators are dangerous

---

A little sulphuric acid,
    Mixed with scrap of zinc,
Heated in a test tube,
    Make an awful—odor.

"MY STARLIGHT MAID."

"Over the Hills," "In the Evening by the Moonlight"
"My Starlight Maid," "How Would You Like to Spoon?"
"I'll be Waiting in the Gloaming"
"In the Shadow of the Pines,"—
"Just One Word of Consolation,"
"Dearie," "Don't you Think It's Time?"
"Somewhere in the World" "Songbirds Are Singing of You,"
"Little Girl You'll Do," "Little Girl you'll Do,"
"Sweetest Maid of All,"
"I'd like to Marry you."

There is a young fellow named Clyde,
Who of our school is the pride.
He sways every student
With laws that are prudent;
Oh, C. A. P., we're all on your side.

Chat—Say, kid, go after that undertaker for an ad.
"Brick"—Yes, that would be fine wouldn't it, and then get up at a rally and ask them to patronize our advertisers.

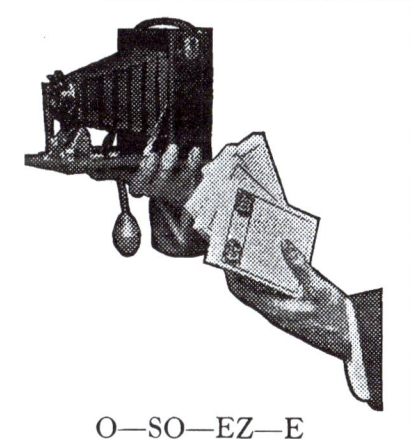
THE DINERS.

The policeman should dine on beets.
The editor on roasts.
The actor on duck-eggs.
The jeweler on carrots.
The machinist on nuts.
The sweetheart on dates.
The wife on tongue.
The husband on pocket-book rolls.

There's a charming young miss
Whom **we** always call "Sis."
Her pet hobby's a curl,
In this fashionable whirl,
Now what do you think of this!

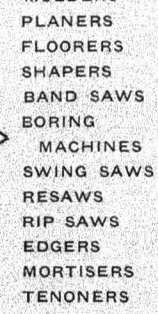

An amendment to the Constitution—a wooden leg.

Student (translating "Das Feuer brennt hell")—The fire burns hot.
Lehrerin—Hell isn't hot.

Merry, mild, but mighty,
In this school sublime,
She is a queen of teachers,
She is a creature divine.

Oh come to the German classroom
To see her as she sways
The bold and dignified Seniors
On with enticing ways.

Serene in her English classroom
Our learned teacher dwells;
Upon our eager ears she pours
The words the gifted poet tells.
How we dote upon her stories
Which, in traveling Europe through
In her memory stamped while viewing,
Countless scenes which History knew,—
Kindling hopes in me and you.

They couldn't seize his baggage because he wore a chest protector.

Preparation for Work

O, YOU CHAMELEON!

The Lick co-ed answered the door-bell. It was HE. She blushed a pretty pink. He kissed her. She blushed a brilliant red. Shh-h! A step in the hallway. It was her father. She turned white with fear. All was silent when brother Willie opened the door and snickered. She was purple with rage. She awoke next morning feeling blue. On the way to school she saw HIM with another damsel. She was green with envy. "Aw, what's the use," said the chameleon as he dug a hole and buried himself.

I keep a bull dog in my yard so the beggars can get a bite outside of the door without asking for it.

If you are on a train, and it's behind time, throw tomatoes on the track to make it catch up.

WITH APOLOGIES.

Doctor Cook, with patient soul
  And many a close shave,
Has placed our flag at the much sought Pole;
  To us, he glory gave.

But such a pole with red, white and blue,
  Has long bedecked our streets;
'Tis there a good, close shave is given, too,
  At the price that all can meet!

H. B. H.. '10.

It's a wise joke that knows its own father.

The man who couldn't express his feelings sent them by slow freight.

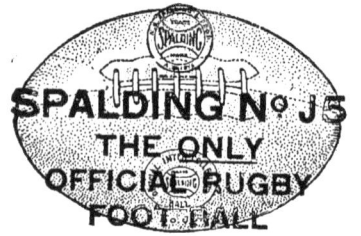

"A Freshman once to Hades went
To see what he could learn,
But soon they sent him back again,
He was too 'green' to burn!"—Ex.

Early to rise,
Early to bed,
These are two things
The Juniors dread.

"Mary had a lot of bees,
And just to save their lives,
The bees all followed Mary,
Because Mary had the hives."—Ex.

Lightning Source UK Ltd.
Milton Keynes UK
UKHW022202260219
338052UK00009B/279/P